THE [illegible] PLACE

BY **SHARR WHITE**

★

★

DRAMATISTS
PLAY SERVICE
INC.

THE OTHER PLACE was originally developed in association with Matt Olin and originally producecd by MCC Theatre (Robert Lupone, Bernard Telsey, William Cantler, Artistic Directors; Blake West, Executive Director) in association with Marc Platt at the Lucille Lortel Theatre in New York City, opening on March 28, 2011. It was directed by Joe Mantello; the set design was by Eugene Lee; the costume design was by Diane Laffrey; the lighting design was by Justin Townsend; the sound design was by Fitz Patton; the video and projection designs were by William Cusick; the production stage manager was B.D. White; and the stage manager was Linda Marvel. The cast was as follows:

JULIANA .... Laurie Metcalf
IAN .... Dennis Boutsikaris
THE WOMAN .... Aya Cash
THE MAN .... John Schippa

CHARACTERS

JULIANA — A sharply charismatic scientist in her early fifties, Juliana's obviously fierce intelligence is both her greatest asset and her largest burden, having helped her carve a niche in a deeply competitive field infiltrated by brilliant minds, and yet bringing her a deep impatience and a drive not always understood by those around her.

IAN — Juliana's husband, early fifties, an oncologist.

THE WOMAN — In her late twenties to early thirties, The Woman portrays: Dr. Cindy Teller, a neurobiologist; Laurel, Juliana and Ian's daughter; and a Woman.

THE MAN — In his late thirties, The Man portrays Richard Sillner, and Bobby, a nurse.

THE SET

This play calls for the use of a minimal stage with projections which then undergoes a sea change into something that feels more like realism. Whether or not sets remain minimal, what is most important is that after this transformation we should feel that at last we are somewhere concrete: This is a scene from the past, and everything we see is now true.

STAGE DIRECTIONS

In the first scenes especially, the pacing of this play should stay crisp, tense and impulsive. To reflect this, stage directions between scenes have been kept minimal.

THE OTHER PLACE

The lights rise on Juliana.

JULIANA. *(Throughout: charming, dry, utterly unsentimental.)* The first glimmer of it comes on a Friday. They've flown me to St. Thomas, some private golf resort, I pretend I'm giving a lecture but really it's another sales pitch, I used to be enthralled by my new life, but the blush has come off the rose. I've landed, checked in, tried Laurel and Richard, taken two aspirin, refused a platter of french toast, forced thirty laps out of myself down at the pool. These last few moments I go through again and again, somehow even with all the knowledge I have — or used to have — I still think I can find some clue as to when it all might have turned, but this is a cruel exercise which I have begun realizing I should avoid. I go up to shower and dress, there is no hurry, everything is on-site, the sea is stunning, the air is seventy one degrees, I am fifty-two years old, in spite of everything that's happened, when I add up the balance sheet of my life the numbers say I am happy. *(The Woman interrupts.)*

DR. TELLER. Ah. Would you like to sit down, Mrs — ?

JULIANA. — Ms., please, I'm going through a divorce.

DR. TELLER. Oh. So … are you no longer going by Smithton?

JULIANA. Yes.

DR. TELLER. Sorry. Let me start over. Your appointment was set up by your —

JULIANA. — Yes, current husband.

DR. TELLER. I see. Do you have the next one picked out?

JULIANA. Next who.

DR. TELLER. Husband.

JULIANA. Well he's not my ex yet, so what do I call him.

DR. TELLER. Right. But the divorce, that's a recent development?

JULIANA. Is this a personal question?

DR. TELLER. Sorry. It's just that when he scheduled you, your hus — I mean … *Dr.* Smithton. Made no mention of that, so I wonder if you're going by a different name.
JULIANA. *(A question.)* My maiden name.
DR. TELLER. *(Writing.)* … Yes. So I'll just make a note and if needed we'll, we'll … re-label your file.
JULIANA. Well why on earth would you have any files started, this is the first time you're seeing me.
DR. TELLER. I have a system.
JULIANA. It's working well. *(The Woman writes. To us, without breaking pace.)* I arrive downstairs, I am greeted with enthusiasm, these are Old Boy events at which women usually do not appear unless to provide some sort of illicit service, and when we do otherwise appear we do not do so in heels, and when we *do* wear heels — unless we immediately prove we are the smartest people in the room — we are not taken seriously. *(Juliana coyly raises a leg. She is wearing a severe, very fashionable pair of heels. Ian appears with two coffee mugs.)*
IAN. Sorry. What?
JULIANA. I said I think any diagnosis should happen at your office.
IAN. My office.
JULIANA. I would just feel more comfortable considering our situation. You want to be separated, we're going to have to be separated; you've got downstairs, I've got upstairs and ne'er the twain shall meet.
IAN. Except for the kitchen, which would be twain, hence we are meeting.
JULIANA. I just think we should separate home life and medical life.
IAN. OK, that's …
JULIANA. What.
IAN. A little strange.
JULIANA. Well I trust you as an oncologist.
IAN. But not as your husband.
JULIANA. You're a better oncologist.
IAN. Gee, thanks.
JULIANA. I would just rather keep this clinical.
IAN. I can maintain a cold demeanor.
JULIANA. Do you think brain cancer is a laughing matter.
IAN. Sorry, I guess I'm a little confused because all I began with was *Do you want coffee.*

JULIANA. … Oh.
IAN. And I was about to add, *And should I make you breakfast. (Small beat.)*
JULIANA. Two eggs over easy, bacon well done. And fruit.
IAN. Uh …
JULIANA. And toast. And a muffin.
IAN. *(Dry.)* Is that all?
JULIANA. And yogurt. With granola. Plus a banana. And then we'll go to your office and you can give me the diagnosis.
IAN. … Except that, look, we're not going to my office, we're seeing Dr. Teller.
JULIANA. And he will what.
IAN. She, right? You saw her last week?
JULIANA. Exactly, and if there's news she'll deliver it, I understand I'm supposed to bring someone to these things. I wish Laurel and Richard weren't so busy.
IAN. Sorry, Laurel and…?
JULIANA. Well Laurel's got the girls because Richard is on the Cambridge trip.
IAN. Laurel's got the girls because Richard is on the Cambridge trip?
JULIANA. I don't want to bother them.
IAN. Well you're going to have *me* this time.
JULIANA. Nonsense, you're leaving me.
IAN. Right.
JULIANA. I wait for everyone to settle, I am introduced, the drinking has already begun, there is a warmer-than-sober round of applause, a flash of yellow catches my eye, as a case in point about women at these things, a girl in nothing but a swimsuit sits among the doctors, she is young, blonde, buoyant, I'm sure she is a prostitute, immediately she gets under my skin. I'm sorry, is this on? *(The Man enters, turns on Juliana's body mic.)*
MAN. *(Into mic.)* Checkity checkity … checkcheckcheck! *(The Man gives a thumbs-up and exits.)*
JULIANA. … Thank you. *(To us.)* I begin the lecture, I say ladies and gentlemen *(Into mic.)* … pardon me, *lady* and gentlemen — I see we have a guest with us today in a lovely string bikini — miss, are you a doctor or are you just here to show someone where it hurts. *(To us.)* Yes, this gets a bit of a laugh and the girl seems embarrassed, I am satisfied. I continue. What, what are you writing. *(The Woman puts her pen down.)*

DR. TELLER. Well let's start there. When you're meeting with me. You'd *prefer* your maiden name?
JULIANA. — Right. And you are …
DR. TELLER. Yes, again, Dr. Teller?
JULIANA. Is that a question.
DR. TELLER. I'm sorry?
JULIANA. You said that with an upward inflection, like you weren't exactly sure who you were.
DR. TELLER. So you *wouldn't* prefer your maiden name.
JULIANA. Oh I would, but it's Liffenberger. How could I go back after Smithton; Juliana Smithton, sounds like I was born with a tennis bracelet. Too bad *Dr.* Smithton can't keep other women's skirts free of his dick.
DR. TELLER. Ah. Uh. So, so, uh, would it be easier then if I, I just … called you Juliana.
JULIANA. This is an old-fashioned line of attack.
DR. TELLER. Attack?
JULIANA. Well it feels like you're preparing for an interrogation.
DR. TELLER. I'm just trying to find out what you're most comfortable with.
JULIANA. May I smoke.
DR. TELLER. Absolutely not.
JULIANA. You could get a smokeless ashtray.
DR. TELLER. Yes, but I couldn't use it on hospital grounds.
JULIANA. Still, a smokeless ashtray, nobody would know, this is a private office, isn't it, you don't share it?
DR. TELLER. And how long have you been smoking.
JULIANA. No idea.
DR. TELLER. Care to think about it?
JULIANA. No I don't think I do.
DR. TELLER. Can you try for me, Juliana?
JULIANA. Yes you may.
DR. TELLER. I'm sorry?
JULIANA. Call me by my first name, thank you so much for asking. *(The Woman writes again.)* What.
DR. TELLER. Have you always been this elusive?
JULIANA. Why would I be elusive, I don't have anything to be guilty about.
DR. TELLER. … I said elusive, not guilty.
JULIANA. *(Into mic.)* Gentlemen. *This … (A projection.)* … is

Identamyl. As most of you know who were smart enough to invest in shares of Spinder & Thompson prior to this final round of clinical trials, Identamyl is perched to become *the* blockbuster protein therapy, with sales projected to exceed one billion dollars by month ten of its debut year alone. My name is Juliana Smithton, I am the advising research scientist and original patent holder of its base structure, though I must issue a note of special thanks to my post-doc, Dr. Richard Sillner, who I regret was not able to be here today. Now. I am going to walk you through this remarkable piece of work before you go hit a bucket of balls into protected sea turtle habitat. *(To us.)* This gets another little chuckle from everyone except for the girl in the yellow bikini; I'm sure I'm glorifying my own power to intimidate but I can swear she suddenly seems … self-conscious by how little she's wearing. I begin to feel a familiar trickle of … regret. *(Raising a cell phone.)* — I said is this Richard. *(The Man raises a phone to his ear. We hear squeals of children in a bath.)*

RICHARD. — Yes! Hello, it's Richard? — Sorry, they're splashing. *(Over his shoulder.) Girls! (Into phone.)* Hang on …

JULIANA. Yes! Richard. It's … it's Juliana, Richard.

RICHARD. *(Miniscule beat.)* Juliana.

JULIANA. Yes, is, is that who I think it is in the background.

RICHARD. Sorry, uh … — Yes, it's bath night, they love the bath, let me get in the other room. *(Over his shoulder.)* Lor, you're watching? *(The Woman calls from offstage.)*

LAUREL. Yeah hon, OK, who is it!

RICHARD. Uh, it's, it's your mother.

LAUREL. — Oh *fuck*ing shit.

RICHARD. *(Into phone.)* Uh. Sorry …

JULIANA. No! No, it's, it's a bad time.

RICHARD. She didn't mean *you*.

JULIANA. It's OK, I know she did.

RICHARD. No, the girls, they, they, they dump water all over the floor.

JULIANA. I know she meant me, Richard.

RICHARD. She, it's, they're not sleeping, that's all, it makes them hyperactive, it's tough …

JULIANA. Well maybe she could just call me later.

RICHARD. Um … Yyyyeah …

JULIANA. — Or … or not. I'll …

RICHARD. — Look. Hey look, why don't you call back, it's, it's just hard to get her to pick up the phone these days, OK?
JULIANA. Don't I know it.
RICHARD. I mean is there … is there any reason…?
JULIANA. — No! Everything's … fine, I mean I'm in a, a hotel, um, in … St. Thomas.
RICHARD. Sounds rough.
JULIANA. Yes, with the new drug actually, finally pitching it, it's going to be a … a big success.
RICHARD. Uh. OK. What am I supposed to say to that, Juliana, gee, you know … congratulations?
JULIANA. No it's just that I've had a bit of an episode and I just … really wanted to hear Laurel's voice.
LAUREL. *(Offstage.)* — Oh! *(A watery THUNK. A girl starts crying.)*
JULIANA. — But I really don't want to keep you. These *are* … *wonderful* years, aren't they.
RICHARD. — Look. I … I received an invitation? To attend a meeting?
JULIANA. Oh! The Cambridge thing!
RICHARD. Biophysical Society?
JULIANA. Oh, well I thought I could help you. Re-establish some connections.
RICHARD. Why, you think my career could ever, what, magically recover? After all the accusations from you and Ian?
JULIANA. Yes well, I … I thought it was time that I start making up for things.
RICHARD. And how could you ever do that.
JULIANA. Look, this is crass, but for starters what about with money. Lots of money. *(Another thunk.)*
LAUREL. — Shit, hon!? Can you hang up on her!?
RICHARD. Uh.
JULIANA. No no, I understand. Why don't I call back in forty five minutes.
✗ RICHARD. … Look. Juliana …
JULIANA. — Next please. *(Projection: A chromosome. Into the microphone.)* Now. For those of you who were only accepted to med school here on St. Thomas, this is called a chromosome. *(To us.)* It's a scientist joke, every doctor is required to laugh at it, and everybody does, except for, again, the girl in the yellow bikini, and though I should leave well enough alone, before I realize it I'm sharp-

ening my claws on her again, I say ... *(Into mic.)* ... now I'm going to make this next part quick so everyone please sit up. Except you, String Bikini, it looks like all you need to work on today is somebody's diction. *(To us.)* This gets a laugh too. But the girl ... reddens. Why do I say it. Why do I say things like this. Why do I see something young and beautiful and want to just scratch it and scratch it until none of it is left. And yet the girl, maybe stubbornly ... doesn't leave. My trickle of regret turns into a flood. *(Ian stands mid-motion, electric razor in-hand.)* You can't stand that I'm reaching out to her.

IAN. Sorry, to?

JULIANA. Laurel ... Laurel. See, this is another one of your problems, you just don't want to let go of everything and move into the future.

IAN. Um. I'll add that to my list.

JULIANA. If there's a Biophysical Society meeting at Cambridge? Great, you should be happy that I'm pulling strings to see that Richard attends.

IAN. — Right. Look. I have to say I'm having a pretty hard time with this.

JULIANA. That's what I'm saying, I'd think you'd be happy I'm finding some way to get *to* them.

IAN. Some way to...?

JULIANA. I mean you can't just say fuck it? They're together? Obviously very together, so what if he's fifteen years older than she is, that mattered a long time ago, but it doesn't anymore, she's an adult.

IAN. What I mean is I really ... *cannot* talk about this.

JULIANA. Fine! Don't! I'll talk, you listen! — What, is that why you're sleeping with somebody else, you can't stand the things I talk about.

IAN. I'm not ... sleeping with somebody else.

JULIANA. — Or maybe you can't stand the tone of my voice or just ... *how* I talk about things, I just think that we're not going to have a shot with our daughter unless you can start accepting *Richard.*

IAN. What the hell could I ever accept about what happened with Richard, Jules.

JULIANA. Well unless we bury the hatchet with *him* there's no way we're going to get her back into our lives. *(Ian is silent.)* You're telling me you have no desire to see the babies.

IAN. OK, Jesus Christ, this isn't funny, I'm going to shave, OK?
JULIANA. I'm serious!
IAN. Yeah, that's what I'm afraid of.
JULIANA. I even thought it might be a good idea to give her the other place.
IAN. Sorry. The…?
JULIANA. I know it's in your name too but hell, it's my family house, she's going to get it once I die anyway, she may as well have it now since we finally know where she is.
IAN. — No no no.
JULIANA. And then they'll just be an hour away.
IAN. … Jules, *please* tell me you're, you're, not in discussion with anyone about … signing over any real estate.
JULIANA. Next. *(Projections: a series of medical slides.)* And as I speak, I … I begin to watch the girl in the yellow bikini out of the corner of my eye, next slide, yes, here we go, unwind human chromosome 19 you will find the gene known as APOE, which produces the *protein* APOE; the main function of genes besides replicating is the production of proteins, and we all know how this happens, next please. Messenger RNA transcribes our gene segment, a ribosome reads the RNA code, a peptide chain is assembled, hits the intracellular environment, next please, and folds up. Much like dough at a carnival hitting hot oil and folding into a funnel cake— hold the powdered sugar. Next, the girl is beginning to fascinate me, not only has she decided to stay and listen to all the medical speak, she is now leaning forward and is actually engaged in what I am saying, almost as if she understands … *everything,* now the folding of this protein will determine its function, this is my field by the way, protein folding, or to be precise … misfolding, and suddenly I think oh God, who is this girl *really*, is she a doctor. Someone. Some invitee. And I begin to actually *wallow* in my regret for insulting her — which, if you haven't figured out by now, is a … well, a very familiar thing for me to do. *(Both Juliana and The Woman hold phones.)*
LAUREL. Are you in the middle of something.
JULIANA. Oh. Oh! Laurel! No, I was just … just lying down for a minute.
LAUREL. Oh well should I …
JULIANA. — No no. No no, it's OK, I'm up now, I'm, I'm standing right up.

LAUREL. Uh. OK, that's great.
JULIANA. But I thought I was going to call *you* back.
LAUREL. Well I had a minute …
JULIANA. Yes but it would be on my dime if I called you back.
LAUREL. Well that's not really how phone calls work any more, right?
JULIANA. *(Digging through her purse.)* Look, let me just find my phone book and I'll call you right back.
LAUREL. Mom, it's no big deal, we're … we're talking already.
JULIANA. Yes, well it would be on my dime!
LAUREL. *(Giving up.)* OK. Look, you know on second thought, it's just too late, I shouldn't have called, I just really wanted to get a glass of wine first.
JULIANA. Oh! You're a wine drinker now.
LAUREL. Um. … Yes, we both are, guzzlers at the moment I hate to say.
JULIANA. Well look I'll send you case of something.
LAUREL. Oh, that's … really not necessary.
JULIANA. Something nice. Well for the twins. I mean — not for them to drink, obviously. — To celebrate.
LAUREL. Well the celebrating part of it's long over.
JULIANA. But if a case of something really great showed up you wouldn't refuse it?
LAUREL. *(Sharp.)* Look, there's nothing we need from you, Mom. *(Suddenly softening.)* Sorry, I'm sorry. I don't mean to be harsh, this is all just … very … awkward. For me. *(Juliana still digs through her purse.)* Uh, are you, are you there?
JULIANA. — Well all I've got in here is blue ballpoint, I can't stand ballpoint, how did I get ballpoint in here.
LAUREL. What, uh, what are you doing.
JULIANA. I can't find my book, can I, and I've got to write down your number but I can't find paper, what's the matter with this hotel, I'll just write it on my *hand* I guess …
LAUREL. OK, it's … it's been utterly surreal, Mom, OK? I'll see you later.
JULIANA. Wait wait wait!
LAUREL. No really, you still don't seem to be able to … focus — that's the wrong word — on me. So I think it's better that I go.
JULIANA. Look I … I called because I wanted you to know that I've … had an episode.

LAUREL. An episode. Of what, television?
JULIANA. My God, you went and got yourself a sense of humor. No, some sort of … how should I know … medical episode. So.
LAUREL. Uh. OK, are … you all right?
JULIANA. Yes I'm perfectly fine, I think it's brain cancer.
LAUREL. What? Brain … *What*?
JULIANA. Relax, relax, I'm not sure yet, I wouldn't let them check me into a hospital here on St. Thomas.
LAUREL. *Where* are you?
JULIANA. It's called St. Thomas, sweetheart — it's one of the *Virgin Islands*.
LAUREL. Gee, really? I thought I'd caught you on top of an actual Catholic saint.
JULIANA. Really, when did you get so funny? Were you this funny before and I just didn't know it?
LAUREL. You're never going to stop being condescending, are you.
JULIANA. No no, I … I wasn't condescending, I meant it that time.
LAUREL. I'm twenty five now, Mom.
JULIANA. Yes, I … I know you are.
LAUREL. Brain cancer? *(Beat.)*
JULIANA. I'd like … to see you. *(On the words* see you*, two small children begin screaming.)*
LAUREL. *(Over her shoulder.)* Richard! Can you get them back in bed! *(Back to phone.)* Sorry Mom, they're up again, what?
JULIANA. I said I'd like to … *(More sudden screaming.)* I'd like to see you, sweetheart!
LAUREL. *(Over her shoulder.)* Richard!
RICHARD. *(Offstage.)* Got it! I got it …
LAUREL. Well I'm on the phone!
JULIANA. You should go.
LAUREL. — No, I … I …
JULIANA. Look, let me send you some money.
LAUREL. Why would you think I need money.
JULIANA. Well, well, *everybody* needs money.
LAUREL. There's no way in hell Richard would take anything from you, you know that, right? *(More screaming.)*
JULIANA. Go, you should go, will you call back.
LAUREL. I … look. I'll … *(More screaming.)*

RICHARD. *(Offstage.)* — Hey *hon?*
JULIANA. Just call me back. Call me back? *(Projections: Medical slides.)* Next please, the girl's eyes get shiny as if she is about to well with tears and I think oh hell, she's not a *doctor* either, she's just someone staying here, in this resort, someone who noticed the placard in the lobby, someone who has had someone close to her die of this, that's why she's here, next please, is it a friend of hers, is it a relative, is it her mother, is she herself predisposed to express this mutation, next please, resulting in the catastrophic cascade of neuron death centered in the hippocampus, many if not most of us have experienced the widespread duress of this disease, the mortality rate of which has been a devastating one hundred percent. Until, just possibly … now.
DR. TELLER. *(Writing.)* Just making a note, good, then let's continue, so you had, uh … an episode.
JULIANA. That's what I'm calling it.
DR. TELLER. … Outside the country.
JULIANA. — United States territory, actually, the Virgin Islands?
DR. TELLER. And no hospital there?
JULIANA. Who the hell would go to a hospital in the Virgin Islands.
DR. TELLER. A few good ones.
JULIANA. Right, for heat stroke and scooter injuries and so I didn't.
DR. TELLER. And so upon getting back your husb … shit … Dr. …
JULIANA. — Soon-to-be-ex —
DR. TELLER. — Yes. Checks you in —
JULIANA. — It's brain cancer.
DR. TELLER. Uh. So, so, and that was a number of weeks ago —
JULIANA. — It's brain cancer —
DR. TELLER. — Right, so I'm beginning with an interview …
JULIANA. Are you not hearing me.
DR. TELLER. I assume you know what a PET scan is?
JULIANA. Who the hell do you think I am.
DR. TELLER. — OK …
JULIANA. And where does Ian come in.
DR. TELLER. Sorry?
JULIANA. — Ian, Ian, my … oh, whatever the hell we're calling him, he's the damned oncologist, divorce or no divorce, he's one of the best.

DR. TELLER. Well, that's, yes, certainly something we're going to look for, just to, to … rule it out.
JULIANA. Look, my whole family died of cancer, Daddy got it in the brain when he was two years younger than I am now, did all sorts of things, got up one morning made scrambled eggs with half a can of dog food. There's one you never forget.
DR. TELLER. And how long did it take for him to uh, uh, to pass.
JULIANA. Well three or four years.
DR. TELLER. *(Writing in Juliana's file.)* Doesn't sound like brain cancer.
JULIANA. Of course it was, chemo kept him alive.
DR. TELLER. Anyone else in your family have this uh, uh, brain cancer?
JULIANA. My father's mother, died around the same age, same thing. *Her* mother died early too apparently, don't know from what.
DR. TELLER. *(Writing furiously now.)* Uh, OK … And can I ask? Do you mind repeating a few words for me?
JULIANA. So this *is* a test.
DR. TELLER. We will do some testing but right now this is still just an interview, car, apple, spigot, can you repeat?
JULIANA. You're not giving me a whatever test.
DR. TELLER. Cognitive?
JULIANA. I'm sorry?
DR. TELLER. Uh, actually, I … I am. *(Projections: medical slides.)*
JULIANA. Next please. Introducing the synthetic molecule Small Interfering RNA-7 Beta. Look at it, it's a thing of beauty. Next please, first theorized by me almost twenty years ago and developed in my lab with the help of Dr. Richard Sillner, SIRNA SEVEN as I patented it, is designed to infiltrate the transcription process and cleave the mutant APOE4 gene, next, halting production of amyloid plaques, and then something happens, next, I let myself … leave my body. Next. I've given this pitch ten times in the last two months, I let myself float above the girl in the yellow bikini, I watch her watching me, next please, why would this young woman cause such loathing in me, such, such … bottomless regret … *(Sharp intake of breath, then, evenly.)* … Oh God. *(Ian appears.)*
IAN. — What, what is it.
JULIANA. *(Feeling her ring finger.)* I've lost it.
IAN. Lost what.

JULIANA. My wedding ring, oh God, well I was putting on lotion and I just set it aside for a minute, it can't just be … *gone.*
IAN. It's right there, Jules.
JULIANA. What? Right where?
IAN. Hon. Where you always put it. In the bowl. Here. *(He lifts a ring out of a little porcelain bowl on the table.)*
JULIANA. I thought for a minute I'd left it back at the other place — in the shower. I keep doing that. *(He stares at her. Tiny beat.)* — Do me a favor and don't ever look at me like that? Please?
IAN. *(Small beat. Then, quietly.)* Come 'ere.
JULIANA. *(Softening, smiling a little.)* No.
IAN. Come over here.
JULIANA. *(Flirtatiously, with a deep love.)* No. *(Ian moves to her. She stares at him. He lifts her hand … and slides the ring on her finger. She closes her eyes. Small beat.)* How can you still love me, Ian.
IAN. I … honestly don't know. God knows I've tried not to, but I just can't stop being crazy about you, isn't that strange. *(They hold one another.)* I'm thinking of suing that resort.
JULIANA. Please, they didn't give me brain cancer.
IAN. It's their fault we had to wait two days to get you to an emergency room.
JULIANA. What good would it have done.
IAN. They let you go back to your hotel room by yourself? Then get on an airplane…?
JULIANA. But that doesn't matter now, I'm here. I'm fine, and you're going to do everything you can to take it out of me.
IAN. If … uh, if it's brain cancer.
JULIANA. Of course it is.
IAN. Look. Cindy's reporting —
JULIANA. — Cindy —
IAN. — Sorry, Dr. Teller —
JULIANA. *(Lightbulb.)* — Cindy?
IAN. Yes, people know her around the hospital, she's well respected.
JULIANA. *Cindyyy.* She's cute, Ian, is she the one?
IAN. Wait wait wait … what?
JULIANA. Do you think she's cute, I think she's fairly cute, guess you don't have to try *that* hard to not love me.
IAN. Jules …
JULIANA. She's a bit young, don't you think, close to Laurel's age, I mean really, you expect your daughter to come out of the

woodwork and meet you when you're doing something as disgusting as dating someone who could practically be one of her friends?
IAN. I'm not … *dating.* Dr. Teller.
JULIANA. Oh, what. I guess just fucking.
IAN. Whoa, whoa, no! We …
JULIANA. — *We,* he says, here it comes …
IAN. No way. No. I …
JULIANA. — Say it.
IAN. I'M TRYING TO! She's a colleague, we've spoken about you over coffee …
JULIANA. So what's the matter, you don't have the balls to go any further, just go fuck her will you please.
IAN. — OK, I, I can't have any more conversations that do this.
JULIANA. — Sure, fine, I'll just put it on the growing list of things you won't talk about any more including your almost total refusal to admit your daughter's very existence!
IAN. Laurel's…? *(Engaging against his better judgment.)* OK, her existence! Fine! Let's go, let's talk about her existence! In fact let's make a bargain, OK? *If* this person calling you is really Laurel …
JULIANA. — Stop it, do you think I'm some doddering old woman — that I'm *falling victim* to some scam artist …
IAN. Well I find it curious this woman has called you a dozen times but she's never called me!
JULIANA. It's *Laurel,* we've spoken, she knows everything, where her room was in the other place, what she likes to eat —
IAN. — And you've had these dozen conversations with her in the three weeks since you returned from St. Thomas after *some sort of an episode* …
JULIANA. — And I've spoken to Richard too, this is unbelievable.
IAN. OK, I guarantee. That you have not been speaking to Richard.
JULIANA. And besides, she was calling me *before* the episode.
IAN. How long before.
JULIANA. How should I know, months.
IAN. And you never told me.
JULIANA. She didn't want me to.
IAN. This is all very convenient.
JULIANA. She's afraid of you!
IAN. Why, I never did anything to make her afraid, at worst I made her … I don't know what. Too bold.

JULIANA. You're the reason she left the house, Ian.
IAN. Don't you lay that at my feet, don't you dare.
JULIANA. Sorry, it's just the way I feel.
IAN. Well your feeling has absolutely no basis in reality! That's what I'm trying to tell you!
JULIANA. — To you, maybe.
IAN. Look. *If* she's really calling you.
JULIANA. She! Is!
IAN. — If there's anyone calling you at *all* …
JULIANA. She's calling me!
IAN. … Then have her contact me. I want to see her. OK? I want her phone number.
JULIANA. Well I don't think she'd like me giving her number out.
IAN. I don't care, I want to see her. And if you cannot make her … materialize …
JULIANA. — Don't you condescend to me!
IAN. … Out of thin air. So that I can speak, *see* her. With my eyes. If you can't. Then you have to stop talking about her.
JULIANA. How could I do that.
IAN. For me. You have to do that. *(Juliana turns back to the audience, ready to continue her lecture, expecting a projection, though now there is none. There is the sense that something somehow has gone wrong.)*
JULIANA. Yes, as I was saying. SIRNA SEVEN is designed to infiltrate the transcription process and … *(Sharp intake of breath, then, evenly.)* … Oh God. *(The Woman appears.)*
DR. TELLER. Maybe you want to tell me a little bit about, about, uh, your … daughter.
JULIANA. Daughter.
DR. TELLER. Dr. Smithton tells me you … have quite an interesting situation on your hands.
JULIANA. Situation.
DR. TELLER. Yes or, or how would you describe it.
JULIANA. Well not as a situation.
DR. TELLER. Yes. So …
JULIANA. — How did *he* describe it.
DR. TELLER. He told me that you're … back in contact. With … her.
JULIANA. May I smoke.
DR. TELLER. Um. Have I been less than clear about smoking here.
JULIANA. You could get a smokeless ashtray.

DR. TELLER. I understand that, but I couldn't use it on hospital grounds.
JULIANA. Still, a smokeless ashtray, nobody would know, this is a private office, isn't it, you don't share it?
DR. TELLER. *(Writing furiously.)* Uh. No. I. I don't share it.
JULIANA. He thinks I'm crazy. That's why he's sending me to you. For some sort of evaluation. You're actually not a doctor at all.
DR. TELLER. *(Still writing.)* I assure you that I am.
JULIANA. That's what all your stupid writing is, you're putting down marks against me.
DR. TELLER. Marks.
JULIANA. Yes, what, you've got two columns there, one for good, one for bad, I keep getting the bad mark.
DR. TELLER. Look. *(Showing Juliana the folder.)* Poorly written misaligned paragraphs. No columns. And those are my diplomas and credentials, there on the wall.
JULIANA. — A little *cliché* don't you think.
DR. TELLER. Yes. A little cliché. *(Beat.)*
JULIANA. My daughter ran away from home.
DR. TELLER. I see.
JULIANA. When she was a teenager. And she never returned.
DR. TELLER. I see.
JULIANA. No I don't think you do. My daughter disappeared. With my post-doc at the time; a boy. Man. Named Richard Sillner. Who was fifteen years her senior.
DR. TELLER. Oh. I … did I … read about that?
JULIANA. Most likely.
DR. TELLER. Were there … very cruel headlines? At the time?
JULIANA. Yes, thank you so much for reminding me of that.
DR. TELLER. Oh. Oh, I'm …
JULIANA. — Look, don't tell me *sorry*, that word exhausts me, I've heard that enough to never want to hear it again, but thank you, I know you're trying to be kind. *(Small beat.)* I saw a photograph once, taken at the turn of last century; a man, Chinese man, attempts to assassinate the emperor, they catch him, display him in a town square, sentence him literally to Death by a Thousand Cuts. They tie him to a scaffold, apply tourniquets to him, amputate his limbs a thousand times. Starting with his fingers and his toes. The photo shows him with about eight inches of each limb left and he's … gazing up into the sky with an …

unspeakable look on his face. Something … beyond agony. Almost beatific. Like he is in such pain that he has transcended pain and is above himself watching himself experience his pain. Losing a child is like that. *(Small beat.)* So then after years of walking around on my own private little scaffold, I get a call, a phone call. And … it's her.

DR. TELLER. Your daughter.

JULIANA. Out of the blue. Believe it?

DR. TELLER. Is … is…?

JULIANA. — Yes. It's her. Do you believe it.

DR. TELLER. It's her?

JULIANA. See, this is what my husband says. Is it her, is it her, I tell him it's her, because it is her, my daughter is calling me. She calls and we have conversations. Short ones. But they *are* conversations. She and Richard are living somewhere, secretly, and they're married with two little girls. My phone rings, I answer it, there she is. I can hear the girls in the background. Sometimes I call *her*. All Ian can say is: Is it her.

DR. TELLER. And what do you say to each other.

JULIANA. We're in negotiations.

DR. TELLER. Over?

JULIANA. Where we can meet. She's jittery, probably a little embarrassed, but I'm not going to ask her any questions, not yet, I don't want to scare her off, I don't even know what name she goes by now, she could hang up and change her number and never call back and I would go through my thousand little cuts all over again.

DR. TELLER. And, and … what sort of negotiations.

JULIANA. I want her to meet me at the other place.

DR. TELLER. The other place.

JULIANA. We have a house, my family house, my great-grandfather built it, on Cape Cod, we spent almost every weekend there, hell, I've been there every weekend for almost my entire life.

DR. TELLER. And … how are they going. Your negotiations.

JULIANA. I think I can get her to meet me there. I don't want to use the cancer as an excuse, but I do want her to know that … that it looks like time is … short. For me.

DR. TELLER. And uh. Can you tell me more about the episode?

JULIANA. Yes.

IAN. Do you know how you can live with something for so long and it changes so slowly that you … adjust?

JULIANA. So I've … just introduced my molecule. And I, I glance behind myself at the screen to make sure I've got the right image.
IAN. Spinder & Thompson, they'd been taping her pitches, and they were surprisingly open about sharing them with me, and uh.
JULIANA. And when I turn back to the audience, the girl in the yellow bikini … *(Sharp intake of breath, then, evenly.)* Oh God.
IAN. Well suddenly all these things she's been doing for, what. *Years.* Just made horrible sense.
JULIANA. Has disappeared. She's vanished into thin air.
IAN. I mean in the lecture she keeps mentioning this post-doc. Richard Sillner, OK? Well Juliana doesn't have post-docs anymore. She doesn't even have a lab. Her full-time job now is promoting this drug.
JULIANA. I mean I would have seen her if she'd walked out, she was sitting in the middle of the room, every single doctor would have stared at her, and I, I, I, I … sort of panic. There's not even an empty chair. She can't just be … gone.
IAN. And as for Richard Sillner, he worked in her lab *ten years* ago. Until we very publicly accused him of … uh … taking our daughter.
JULIANA. And then I realize uh, uh, uh, that this phrase. *She can't just be gone*. Is very familiar. When Laurel disappeared it was perhaps the only thought I had for … months.
IAN. Except that Richard Sillner didn't take our daughter.
JULIANA. She can't just be gone. She can't just be gone. She *can't* just be …
IAN. I mean in the tape it's so weird, she just …
JULIANA. … And then I realize I am no longer speaking.
IAN. … Stops.
JULIANA. It's as simple as that. And I have no idea how *long* I've not been speaking, just that the room is silent and all these men are staring at me and the only thing I can hear is *she can't just be gone*.
IAN. And you can see it on the tape, all the blood drains out of her face. And she scrabbles around a little with her notes as if she's … totally lost.
JULIANA. And I think to myself, my God, am I having a stroke, except that I'm oddly not able to locate the word *stroke*, so it's more like *my God am I having a thingy?* Finally I, I manage to say … I'm terribly sorry, this is terribly strange, I've … suddenly become a little ill and must break this lecture off midway, my deepest apologies.

IAN. And really, almost as one entity, every doctor in the room leaps to his feet. And I guess it alarms her because she turns vicious.
JULIANA. It's really quite touching.
IAN. She begins screaming — *screeching.*
JULIANA. I'm very calmly telling them it's the flying, I've been flying a lot, can someone help me to my room.
IAN. She runs to the front desk screaming that they're after her, where is her room, can someone find her room, frankly I can see everyone deciding my wife is just a, a, a, crazy person — certainly you could *argue* the point, right? I mean this Richard Sillner guy she keeps mentioning …
JULIANA. And, and, and … I get up to my room. And I have a little rest. And I call Laurel and Richard.
IAN. Uh. You see, Richard … it's complicated … died. OK? Five — six — years ago. I … we read about it. Uh. His suicide. *(A significant beat: something has shifted. Ian helps Juliana into her coat.)*
JULIANA. I'm sorry, you need to prepare me … for what.
IAN. For the fact that we're not going to my office at the hospital today because I'm, I'm not actually your doctor, Jules.
JULIANA. Of course you are, don't be ridiculous.
IAN. Dr. Teller is your doctor.
JULIANA. You mean *Cindyyy.*
IAN. However you wish to refer to her.
JULIANA. Why would *Cindy* be my doctor, she's not an oncologist, is she?
IAN. Right. Which is why I just want to prepare you for the idea that … that this probably isn't brain cancer.
JULIANA. It's not what?
IAN. It's not brain cancer, sweetheart. *(Beat. Juliana stares at him.)*
JULIANA. Shouldn't that be *good* news.
IAN. *(Grim.)* Yes. *(Juliana takes out a cigarette.)* Whoa whoa whoa whoa.
JULIANA. You don't mind, do you?
IAN. What, what're you doing?
JULIANA. I'm smoking.
IAN. You're what?
JULIANA. I'm going to light this cigarette on fire and breathe the smoke from it into my lungs.
IAN. You're, you're … *smoking* again?
JULIANA. Oh, don't be such a Pollyanna.

IAN. When did you …
JULIANA. — Well I'm getting lonely; since you've filed for divorce I no longer have anything intimately approaching my mouth.
IAN. Jesus Christ, Jules, we just had sex last night.
JULIANA. Oh don't be such a contrarian.
IAN. *(Calm.)* And I haven't filed for a divorce, nor am I going to.
JULIANA. Oh don't be such a wimp.
IAN. And *you're* the one who wanted me to move downstairs, OK, I just want that stated for the record.
JULIANA. Oh don't be such a bureaucrat.
IAN. I'm sorry, are … are we mocking me? Is that what we're doing?
JULIANA. — Oh don't be such a …
IAN. — Jules. Can you stop it.
JULIANA. I'm just having a little fun, you should let me have a little fun before you tell me I've got seven hours left to live or something, so don't be such a …
IAN. — What. Don't be such a what.
JULIANA. I can't think of any more.
IAN. So the smell up there, it's not actually coming in from the neighbor's window like you said it was.
JULIANA. You might also be smelling burnt filter, I've set a personal goal of smoking each one of my cigarettes right down to the nub.
IAN. Terrific.
JULIANA. Yes, in every single room including your *home* office, which I think you'll be happy to know is now my official smoking room.
IAN. You know what surprises me almost more than anything else? Is how … cruel this thing has made you.
JULIANA. What thing. *(Beat.)* What thing, Ian. *(Beat.)* Perhaps I express cruelty because I've got a husband who won't admit that his daughter exists no matter how much I beg him to believe me. And because I believe that if he loved me as much as he is supposed to love me he will do his best to believe in the depths of his heart that his daughter has made contact with me. And that it is only a matter of time before I can convince her to come home. So may I smoke.
IAN. Smoke, smoke; smoke your fucking guts out, what the hell difference does it make.

JULIANA. Should I interpret that as some terrible uh-oh. *(A small beat, he nods again. Juliana lights a cigarette.)* Well if it bothers you so much we should get a few …
IAN. … A few what.
JULIANA. Well a few of those things.
IAN. What things.
JULIANA. For the whatever.
IAN. For the whatever what.
JULIANA. For the stuff. That falls from the thing.
IAN. From the cigarette? The ashes, for the ashes? A couple of ashtrays?
JULIANA. Yes, but without the smoke.
IAN. We should get some *smokeless* ashtrays?
JULIANA. Yes, some of those.
IAN. Juliana?
JULIANA. *(Quietly.)* Just give me the news.
IAN. *(Quietly.)* Hell, give me a drag of that. *(Small beat. Juliana hands over the cigarette. Silence.)*
JULIANA. How bad am I.
IAN. They sliced your imaging every which way. Frontal lobe, parietal, even temporal, nothing.
JULIANA. At all?
IAN. No tumors.
JULIANA. They'll find something.
IAN. They did see some … elevated, uh. Glucose levels. Uh. In the hippocampus. *(Long, terrible pause while this sinks in.)*
JULIANA. Bullshit.
IAN. So she's looking into several … dementias, which would explain a lot.
JULIANA. A lot of what!
IAN. What's funny is that *you're* the expert on this.
JULIANA. Bull. Shit.
IAN. Look, I'm just telling you what she's told *me*, do you want me to try and interpret that or not.
JULIANA. Not, absolutely not, you're a fucking hack, Ian.
IAN. Really? Gee it's funny because I'm pretty widely regarded as one of the best.
JULIANA. Yes, but you're a fucking *oncologist*, you don't know anything about dementia, that's like letting a proctologist look at your heart.

IAN. Considering your treatment of me lately that's where I might recommend looking for yours.
JULIANA. Well aren't you just a bag of laughs. I mean if I had dementia, I would know about it, don't you think, I've been studying goddamned dementia all my life, I'm fifty-two, I don't have *dementia*, what *sort* of dementia, do I sound *demented* to you?
IAN. — That's what I'm saying sweetheart, you, you really do.
JULIANA. BULLSHIT!
IAN. *(Quietly.)* She'd like to test more.
JULIANA. More *what*, I'm sorry, what is this thing you're calling a *test*, I'm feeling *demented!*
IAN. I spoke to some colleagues, everyone's tempted to say it's early stage but these other things you're doing, especially since St. Thomas …
JULIANA. What colleagues! *Cindyyyyy?* This is bullshit, I had a … a … FUCK!
IAN. A what, you had a what.
JULIANA. … A … a … a … a THINGY.
IAN. A thingy?
JULIANA. Yes! When you're, you're, you've …
IAN. I. DON'T. KNOW. *(Beat.)* I don't recall you ever saying anyone in your family … had … uh … *(Small beat.)*
JULIANA. *(Quietly.) I* don't have … *(Small beat.)* I don't have it Ian. *(The Woman appears. Ian stays.)*
DR. TELLER. So. Of course as you know, uh, uh, early-onset is still very hard to diagnose while a patient is still alive.
JULIANA. Well why don't I make it easier for us and jump off the fucking roof.
IAN. *(Softly.)* Jules …
DR. TELLER. Are you … flirting with suicidal thoughts, Juliana?
JULIANA. Dating them actually. But they won't put out.
IAN. Oh good lord.
JULIANA. *(Already lighting another cigarette.)* May I smoke.
DR. TELLER. *(Reaching for it.)* Absolutely not.
JULIANA. GET THAT GIRLIE FACE AWAY FROM ME! BEFORE I BURN YOUR EYES OUT!
IAN. *(Sharper.)* Jules.
DR. TELLER. … OK.
JULIANA. *(Re: Ian.)* And what the hell is he doing here, he's goddamned divorcing me.

IAN. Please. Sweetheart. I drove you here.
JULIANA. *(To The Woman.)* You didn't tell me this.
DR. TELLER. Uh. Right, I didn't think it was necessary, seeing as ... he drove you here.
JULIANA. *(To Ian.)* Where from, the other place? *(Small beat. Ian and The Woman share a look.)* What, for Christ's sake.
IAN. *(Stands.)* Sorry. You know what? I'm sorry, I think I have to stop.
DR. TELLER. Look. Yes. I understand, this really is happening with, uh, uh, uncommon speed—
IAN. — Right! Yes! So let's, let's ... please. Just stop. For a minute.
JULIANA. Oh. I almost forgot. Sweetheart, could you run out and see if Laurel's here yet, she's driving out to meet me.
IAN. Uh, OK, there's no fucking way ...
DR. TELLER. — But the most important thing you can do right now is to keep in mind our discussions, OK?
JULIANA. What the hell is she talking about.
IAN. I don't want to keep anything in mind, I just want this to stop. I want it to stop.
DR. TELLER. Ian, I want us all to take a breath and focus everything we have on next steps, OK, beginning with —
JULIANA. — One minute. *(Juliana takes out her own small pad and paper and starts writing.)*
DR. TELLER. Good, yes, please, write these down.
JULIANA. *(Still writing.)* Well *you're* making secret notes, why shouldn't I?
DR. TELLER. No, I, I highly recommend you write out everything you can.
JULIANA. Here's something you may want to explain, it says here someone named Cindy is having sex with my husband—
IAN. — Jules—
JULIANA. — Is that you?
DR. TELLER. OK, that would, would be totally incorrect.
JULIANA. *(Scribbling.)* So you're not sucking his dick.
IAN. *Please*, Jules!
JULIANA. *(Scribbling.)* One moment, please. *Sucking. Ian's* ...
IAN. I SAID GODDAMN IT JULES, PLEASE!
DR. TELLER. Ian.
JULIANA. What's *he* shouting about? *(Ian suddenly sobs.)* Oh for heaven's sake.

IAN. Sorry. I'm sorry! God.
JULIANA. Oh Ian, stop it, I should be the one crying, not you!
IAN. Give me a minute.
JULIANA. Really, you've got the most horrible way of making everything all about you, don't you.
IAN. CAN YOU GIVE ME A MINUTE! CAN YOU DO THAT! I'M JUST NOT READY FOR THIS! I'M NOT READY FOR ANY OF THIS! *(Silence. He blows his nose.)*
JULIANA. Finished. *(He nods.)* Good, that settles it then, we'll reschedule and I'll just get going.
DR. TELLER. Sit down, Juliana.
JULIANA. Laurel's got to be waiting out there by now.
IAN. Laurel is not waiting out there.
JULIANA. Don't be ridiculous, she's driving me back to the other place.
IAN. WE SOLD THE OTHER PLACE, JULES!
JULIANA. Are you feeling OK, sweetheart? — He's acting totally demented.
IAN. We sold it ten years ago when Laurel disappeared, we couldn't stand to be out there any more —
JULIANA. — He's never going to admit she's come back to me.
IAN. PLEASE, JULES, PLEASE, PLEASE!
DR. TELLER. IAN!
JULIANA. She's at the other place, she's at the other place, she's at the other place … *(Continuing this quiet chant through the following.)*
IAN. LAUREL IS DEAD SOMEWHERE! SHE HITCHHIKED IN FRONT OF OUR HOUSE AND SOME FUCKER TOOK HER AND SHE'S FUCKING DEAD! BURIED IN SOME DITCH! OR CUT INTO PIECES AND DUMPED INTO THE SOUND! She has not come back, she is not calling you, she is not married to Richard, they do not have little twin girls, I am not leaving you, we no longer live in the other place …
JULIANA. *(Closing her eyes, quietly.)* … she's at the other place, she's at the other place, she's at the other place, she's at the other place …
IAN. Juliana. Jules.
JULIANA. *(Now almost whispered.)* … the other place, the other place, the other place, the other place, the other place, the other place … *(The lights change. Juliana is left standing alone, with her eyes closed, whispering to herself. We hear a crash of surf, the shishing*

of incoming water over sand, a brief gravity-defying pause, and then, a crushing, cataclysmic roar as thousands of cobblestones are ground against one another by the inescapable backwash of the sea. Blackout. As the lights rise again the mood of the stage is transformed. The space feels warmer, more naturalistic, and we are aware that there has been a change in time. We hear rain. Juliana is on the phone, a cold compress held up to the other side of her face.) (On phone.) — Crisis. *(Impatient.)* — *Crisis. (Spelling.)* — C.R.I. ... Yes, crisis, you really should be able to understand the word crisis if you're an answering service for a shrink. — No I don't want to tell *you* about it, I want you to relay to *him* that my daughter — that his patient ... OK, this is unbelievable. — *Crisis!* — *Yes!* And can he please call our Cape Cod number ... — OK, I am not saying it again, you are a complete idiot. *(Juliana hangs up, and then stands still, listening intently and very worriedly. Ian enters in a dripping wet rain slicker, carrying a briefcase.)*
IAN. *(Wearily irritable.)* OK? Finished. All right? Got him in the car, watched him go. — *That* was the most unpleasant thing I've ever done.
JULIANA. *(Listening, silencing him with a finger.)* — Waitwait, listen. *(Tense silence. Juliana listens. So does Ian. Rain spatters the windows.)*
IAN. Jules?
JULIANA. — Shh! *(A beat. They both listen again.)*
IAN. OK, I give up, what are we listening for.
JULIANA. *(Very worried.)* She's still in her room, right?
IAN. How would I know, I've been here for six minutes.
JULIANA. — Look, can you just go up and check on her, OK?
IAN. And say what, I have no idea what's going on around here.
JULIANA. *Please* go up and check, there's no way I can go up there. *(Juliana listens, quite desperately. A beat. Ian makes a helpless gesture, then turns and exits.)*
IAN. *(From offstage, a little bewildered.)* Uh. Laurel? *(Silence.)* Laurel, are you in there? *(Silence.)* Can you ... Can you come down, sweetheart? I'd ... I guess I'd like to talk to you about ... whatever the hell's happening *this* time. *(A beat. We hear a door slam. At the sound of this, Juliana registers a profound relief. Thrumming classical music begins, played at mammoth levels, but deeply within the house so that it sounds both thundering and faint. Ian reenters. He stares at Juliana.)* Happy? She's put on the ... whatever.

JULIANA. Gustav Mahler.

IAN. … Again. I always hoped she'd be a punk rocker. But no, she's got to be — what is she, a, a … *classicist.*

JULIANA. A classicalist.

IAN. A classical romantic. … ist. *(A small beat. Juliana, pulls the compress from her face to reveal a violent, blossoming bruise.)* Holy shit, Jules. OK, am I, am I … calling anyone? Cops? Uh … ambulance?

JULIANA. *(Weakly, buried in his shoulder.) No.*

IAN. Did this Richard guy do this?

JULIANA. No.

IAN. *Laurel* did this?

JULIANA. I'm trying to call Dr. Wollman.

IAN. The shrink? *(Juliana nods.)* Because two hundred bucks a week is obviously paying off. — I'll be right back.

JULIANA. *(Trying to stop him.)* Ian … !

IAN. *(Offstage, over the music.)* LAUREL?

LAUREL. GO! AWAY!

IAN. LAUREL GODDAMN IT TURN THAT CRAP OFF AND COME OUT! NOW! OPEN THIS FUCKING DOOR RIGHT NOW BEFORE I KICK THE FUCKING THING IN!

LAUREL. I'M NOT COMING OUT AS LONG AS SHE'S IN THIS HOUSE, SO FUCK OFF! I SAID FUCK! OFF!

LAUREL. *(An offstage door* does *open, and we hear loud and clear. With outraged, adenoidal conviction.)* AND IT'S NOT *CRAP* BY THE WAY IT'S FUCKING *MAHLER* HE'S THE GREATEST COMPOSER OF *ALL TIME! (The door slams again. Silence. We hear the crashing of surf. Ian reenters, a bit shocked himself. Beat.)*

IAN. *(Dry.)* You're right. She's a total classicalist.

JULIANA. — Ow. Don't make me laugh.

IAN. *(Looking down at himself.)* Fucking shit. Got water all over the house.

JULIANA. Doesn't matter.

IAN. *(Taking off his slicker.) Still* can't have anything nice. Get the new dining table, mysterious burn marks appear, get the new car, she rubs it against a stop sign, re-do the floors —

JULIANA. — Ian. *(As if to prove Ian's point, the music suddenly starts again. Ian throws his hands up. Small beat.)*

IAN. OK. Start talking, hon.
JULIANA. It's … a blur.
IAN. Uh. Well you'd better un-blur it because when I pull up —
JULIANA. — I'm *sorry* —
IAN. — to find you shouting at me to get your lab assistant —
JULIANA. — Post-doc —
IAN. — Whatever, "the fuck into his car and away from our house" …
JULIANA. — I found him in her room. *(Small beat.)*
IAN. Uh. OK, how much in her room.
JULIANA. It's really a blur.
IAN. The sort of *in her room* where somebody's clothes were off? Were *her* clothes off?
JULIANA. What part of *blur* do you not understand.
IAN. You can't tell me if their clothes were off? She's, she's *fifteen* years old.
JULIANA. *(Overlapping.)* Their clothes were not off!
IAN. *(Overlapping.)* I mean is he, is he, I don't know, *weird?*
JULIANA. — He's a *scientist*, Ian, he's *weird.*
IAN. Thought this crap was over and done with, last thing I imagined tonight was coming home to, to … *(Juliana presses on her cheekbone.)* right. Unbelievable. Come here. *(Juliana leans her cheek towards him. He examines her.)*
JULIANA. Do you think she broke it?
IAN. *(Examining.)* You generally know when something's broken.
JULIANA. Ow! Ian!
IAN. Yeah, looks like just a bad bruise.
JULIANA. She just … Whap. Whap. Like that.
IAN. Sorry, I guess I don't understand what happened, she just … *turned* on you?
JULIANA. Ian! It's! A blur! *(The phone rings.)* — Thank God, that's the shrink.
IAN. Well if he's looking for a piece of somebody's mind, he can talk to me.
JULIANA. *(Answering.)* — Dr. Wollman? *(Beat.)* — Hello? — Is this Dr. Wollman? *(Small beat. Juliana hangs up. Ian looks puzzled.)*
IAN. What is it.
JULIANA. No. Nothing. … Music's off. *(Juliana and Ian share a glance. Ian moves to the door and calls upstairs.)*
IAN. Laurel? Laurel. *(The music is turned back on. Small beat.)*

JULIANA. — Oh my God, my, my head … is spinning.
IAN. Are you … OK?
JULIANA. I don't know, I've got to sit.
IAN. *(Sitting her down.)* — Do you want something? Water?
JULIANA. Do you think there's something wrong with me?
IAN. Yeah, I think you don't keep your guard up.
JULIANA. I don't mean like that.
IAN. — I think there's something wrong with *her*. I think this shrink thing is a noble idea, but come on, she's *assaulted* you this time, this is an attack …
JULIANA. That's not what I'm talking about. *(Ian exits.)*
IAN. *(Calling from offstage.)* — Or would you rather have a scotch or something?
JULIANA. No, just … just water. *(Ian remains offstage. We watch Juliana closely as she listens to him.)*
IAN. *(Offstage.)* … And I mean holy crap, the things he was shouting out there, calling you a, a psychopath? Calling you a, some … a *rager* was the word he used, what does he mean *rager?*
JULIANA. Someone who … has rages. Probably. *(Ian enters with a scotch for himself and a glass of water for Juliana.)*
IAN. Here … and then do have a little scotch, OK, it's bracing — I know that sounds very *nineteenth century*.
JULIANA. I come home with the fish, I, I, close the door, and when I turn back into the house, up there in the hall, I see him open her door and walk *out* of her room then go into the bathroom and shut *that* door.
IAN. Uh. OK …
JULIANA. And so I wait for him to come out of the bathroom and I— OK, pretty sharply — ask him just what the fuck he thinks he's doing in her bedroom, and then *she* comes out, and, and …
IAN. And what.
JULIANA. — I mean who else does what I do for their post-docs? *I* know It's a hard life for them; I've got a house at the beach, right? So please, stay weekends, enjoy it …
IAN. — Jules? And then *she* comes out and … *(The phone rings again. Juliana and Ian glance at each other. Is this odd?)*
JULIANA. *(Picking up.)* — Hello, who is this please. *(Small beat.)* — Dr. Wollman? *(Dawning.)* — Or Richard. Is that who this is?
IAN. — Is it him?

JULIANA. *(Waving Ian off.)* If this is you Richard, let me tell you a few things. Do not call here again. Do not come by. Do not come by the lab. You are fucking fired. And in fact, if I see you come by this house, if I even see any *evidence* of you having been here, I will fucking kill you —
IAN. — whoa, whoa —
JULIANA. *(To Ian.)* I will, I'll kill him. *(To the phone.)* I will fucking kill you Richard, do you understand me! *(Juliana hangs up, hard. Ian stares.)* What. *(Small beat. Off Ian.)* What!
IAN. Take it easy, hon.
JULIANA. Don't tell me to take it easy!
IAN. You could get in a lot of trouble for that, you can't tell somebody you're going to kill them.
JULIANA. I mean it *metaphorically.*
IAN. *(Tiny beat.)* Really.
JULIANA. Oh shut up, Ian. *(Small beat. Juliana leaves the room.)*
IAN. Juliana?
JULIANA. *(Offstage.)* YEAH? IS THAT YOUR FUCKING BOYFRIEND CALLING THE HOUSE?
LAUREL. FUCK! *YOU!*
JULIANA. *(Offstage.)* DID YOU HEAR WHAT I SAID TO HIM? DID YOU?
LAUREL. *(Sobbing, overlapping.)* FUCK YOU FOR FUCKING EVER! *(A beat. The music turns on again. Juliana comes back in; spent, perhaps a little afraid of what she has just said.)*
IAN. *(Quietly aghast.)* Jules?
JULIANA. She told me she had sex with him. *(All the blood drains out of Ian's face.)* Right. OK?
IAN. With … with … *(Juliana nods.)* Why didn't you …
JULIANA. Because she, she may actually not have.
IAN. Sorry. Did she have sex with him, or didn't she.
JULIANA. I mean she, she, screamed "*I fucked him.*" You know. Right into my face — *(Off Ian.)* now hold on, I don't want any overreacting.
IAN. Really! Overreacting!
JULIANA. She also screamed it … after I went into her room … *(Small beat.)* … and shut the door behind me and … and chased her. Uh. Into a corner.
IAN. Chased her into a corner.
JULIANA. Which … might … be why … Richard is saying that

I'm a rager, he, he, was standing right out there in the hall, and well I … chased her around the room until she huddled up in the corner. Uh, near her dresser, and, and, she … covered herself up with her hands. And then I, I … suppose I was … screaming at her. And that's when she screamed back at me … probably to be as hurtful as she could … that she fucked him.

IAN. And then? *(Beat.)* Jules?

JULIANA. And then I hit her.

IAN. You…?

JULIANA. I, I hit her.

IAN. Before or after she hit you.

JULIANA. Before. And I told her that I … that I wanted her out of my house. Tonight. *(Silence. Juliana realizes something.)* Music's stopped. *(Juliana stiffens. They listen. Silence. Ian glances at Juliana and moves quietly to the stairs. Silence.)*

IAN. *(Calm.)* Laurel? *(He ascends. Juliana listens for all she's worth. Silence. From offstage.)* Hey Jules? Uh … *(Small beat.)* She's not down *there*, is she? *(To Jules.)* Juliana! Is she *down* there!

JULIANA. *(Sharp intake of breath.)* — Oh God! *(Juliana is frozen.)*

IAN. *(Offstage.)* LAUREL!? *(Calling from offstage.)* OK, she must have left! — Laurel?!— I'm … I'm going out! Right now! You stay there, OK, you wait for her to come back, OK? — LAUREL? *(We hear keys, footsteps, a front door shutting. Dimly, we hear Ian calling into the night.) Laurel? Laurrrrrelllll! (Again, the roar of waves on the beach. Juliana is at the peak of realizing what has just happened. The lights change. The Woman steps into the room. She carries a dripping umbrella and a bag of Chinese takeout.)*

JULIANA. *(A small, almost silent sigh of the deepest yearning imaginable.) Ohhhhhhhhhhhhhh.*

THE WOMAN. *(Shocked, a little scared.)* Uh. H … hello? *(Juliana runs to The Woman and throws her arms tightly around her. Over Juliana.)* OK. Whoa. Whoa. Whoa … *(Continued, overlapping, stopping where appropriate.)*

JULIANA. I'm sorry! I'm sorry, sweetheart, I'm so sorry! I didn't mean it, I didn't mean any of it! We looked for you, we looked so hard for you, the police, the FBI, we had hundreds of people looking for you, we combed the beach, we looked in the water, I took a year off and looked for you, how did you hide from me, how did you do it … *(Letting The Woman silence her.)*

THE WOMAN. *(Overlapping, stiffly, more commanding than comforting.)* Stopstopstop. Shh Shh Shh. Stopstopstop. Shh Shh Shh.
JULIANA. *(Pulling away form the woman.)* — Oh God you still have all of your things, let me help you with your …
THE WOMAN. *(Overlapping; brusque, dodging Juliana's grasp.)* Nono. Please nono. I don't need help.
JULIANA. *(Still quite breathlessly.)* — Are you coming from somewhere. — Are you coming from work. — Did you have a long drive.
THE WOMAN. *(Overlapping just a little.)* No no. That's enough. No no.
JULIANA. — Do you want to stay in your old room. — Or we have the guest room!
THE WOMAN. *(Again.)* No no. Sh sh. Yes, I'm going to just set these down but please do not help me.
JULIANA. — Sorry. — I'm sorry. It's been so long. I'm sorry.
THE WOMAN. *(Setting her things down.)* Yes. It's. Sure. Been a long … time, uh, as in I really think you're a, a, a, a little. Uh. Lost.
JULIANA. — Oh don't tell me I have the wrong day. *(Getting upset.)* God oh God, I have the wrong day …
THE WOMAN. — No no, there's no crying. I mean yes I think actually you have the wrong *house,* but I can't have a strange person here crying.
JULIANA. We said to meet *here*, I wrote it down, I've got it in my book, where the hell is my book.
THE WOMAN. — OK how's this. Is. Is anyone. Uh. *With* you. Is anyone looking for you. Can I, can I, help you *find* someone.
JULIANA. Well I snuck out. I mean your father, he … he still doesn't believe me, but … *here you are.*
THE WOMAN. Or maybe there's someone I can call. For you. So they can come and take you out of my house. Uh, right now. How about that. *(The woman's phone rings.)* Oh God, OK, I have to take this, but please while I'm speaking, no … no touching me. *(Answering immediately, not taking her eyes off Juliana.)* — Cheryl hi, um, um, I, I have not, uh, done the walkthrough yet, I, I, there's, a … situation here, um, there's a *woman* here … No, not one of Frank's girlfriends, Frank it would appear has indeed left the house as agreed but uh, uh, I'm … I'm going to call you back. *(She hangs up. Beat. Juliana stares.)*
JULIANA. You're … so … *beautiful.*
THE WOMAN. OK. Uh. Again. Who can I call for you.
JULIANA. And you're so … tall.

THE WOMAN. *(Taking off her hat.)* Yes that's the, the, heels, they make you look like the tallest fucking woman on earth, uh.
JULIANA. And you're so skinny, how did you get so damned skinny.
THE WOMAN. *(Half to herself, not quite hiding bitterness.)* Not skinny enough any more, apparently.
JULIANA. You're almost too skinny, you look so beautiful, you don't think you look beautiful?
THE WOMAN. *(Mostly to herself.)* OK, a stranger has broken into my house and is now talking about my weight. Who am I calling.
JULIANA. — Oh my God I've forgotten about Richard and the girls. — Are they still in the car? — Are they *sitting* out there? — They've got to come in. — I can go out. — Yes I'll go out. — Does he not want to bring them in? — He doesn't want them to see me. — God does this mean you're not going to stay.
THE WOMAN. No no. No no I said. Shush please. Uh. Richard and the girls. Are. Are, not here. They … didn't, uh, come. Tonight. How about that. *(The woman's cell phone rings.)* Crap. *(Answering.)* — Frank, you're not supposed to be calling me directly, I thought we'd agreed on that. — Look I, I, I … can't talk about this right now. — Well you need to call your guy who will call Cheryl who will then give me any message. — FRANK, I'M NOT … I'm not going to talk about anything like this with you any more I have to go. *(Hanging up.)*
JULIANA. Was that Richard. What is he doing, is he looking after the girls.
THE WOMAN. Uh. OK. Yes. Richard. Is looking after the girls so he just couldn't make it, look, I'm … I'm sorry. This is not really in my weekend plan, OK, I've got to do a walkthrough, make sure the prick hasn't ruined anything during *his* weekend, and then I have to drink so much white wine that I will spontaneously relax and I really want this to happen without some very confused woman I don't know trying to give me a hug.
JULIANA. But can't you just call Richard and tell him to bring the girls? And you can all stay? *All weekend?*
THE WOMAN. — OK, you know what? I *am* going to shove you out the door, time's up in my house, you can go be crazy somewhere else —
JULIANA. — What? —
THE WOMAN. — That's right, sorry, this is officially too weird for me, I need you to go, I'm going to give you my eighty-dollar

umbrella as a consolation prize.
JULIANA. But but but … *why?*
THE WOMAN. Because it's a really nice umbrella and I feel bad, but please, this is my house! I worked too hard to get this house every other stupid weekend to not enjoy every stupid second of it, so you have to go, I can't do this, I'm sorry!
JULIANA. Laurel …
THE WOMAN. That's not my name.
JULIANA. Laurel?
THE WOMAN. — That's not my name! Get outta here, lady! I mean it!
JULIANA. — Don't do this —
THE WOMAN. — Let's go, let's get your purse, and your keys, and, and—
JULIANA. *(Getting quite upset.)* — Don't do this, don't do this! Don't do this!— *(Covering her face with her hands.)* — Don't don't don't don't don't don't don't don't don't don't don't don't …
THE WOMAN. Oh hell. *(Then soothing.)* Hey. Hey … *(Taking her gently by the arms.)* It's OK. It's OK, everything's OK. *(Juliana suddenly throws her arms around The Woman again.)* Oh … kay. Hugging. Again. Well. All right. It's … *(Beginning to actually comfort her.)* Shhhhhhh. It's all right.
JULIANA. Please don't leave me.
THE WOMAN. … I … I …
JULIANA. Please. Just tell me you won't leave me.
THE WOMAN. I … *(A beat.)* I won't leave you.
JULIANA. I'm terribly confused.
THE WOMAN. … OK, can you sit? Can I … can I get you to … sit? *(They sit. A beat.)* All right? *(Small beat.)*
JULIANA. *(Meekly.)* I'm … having a hard time figuring out … where I am.
THE WOMAN. Should I … help you with that? *(A small beat. Juliana nods.)* OK, can you … tell me your name?
JULIANA. Why can't you just call me Mom.
THE WOMAN. Oh … *(To herself.)* … Shit.
JULIANA. What, what is it.
THE WOMAN. I've got an idea. *(The Woman rises and goes to Juliana's purse.)*
JULIANA. What are you doing in my purse! *(The Woman finds Juliana's wallet and flips it open.)*

THE WOMAN. How about I call you … Juliana. How's that.
JULIANA. Well, I think that's a little *weird.*
THE WOMAN. *(To herself.)* Good, and a contact number. *(Noticing Juliana's things strewn around the table.)* Wait a minute. Juliana, how long have you been here.
JULIANA. Oh, all my life.
THE WOMAN. I mean … hours? *Days*? Neither of us comes out during the week— though I know Frank's coming out on *his* weekends because of the, the, lipstick on the glasses … *(Juliana has started rummaging through The Woman's bag of Chinese food.)* … uh, OK, yes … help yourself, there's noodles and dumplings and egg rolls and soup. And kung pao chicken and sweet and sour shrimp and mu shu, I'm, I'm … doing like a lot of emotional eating right now?
JULIANA. What's *emotional eating.*
THE WOMAN. *(As she dials.)* Just like it sounds, I don't know why I do it, it only makes everything worse.
JULIANA. Everything what, sweetheart.
THE WOMAN. It's a long story I'm not going to tell you about. — Yes, hi. I'm calling about … *(A glance at Juliana.)* — Yes! Juliana, oh good, thank God, yes I am, she's right here, uh, in my house. And you're…? — Well, no wonder, you must be so worried. *(Juliana has found a large bottle of water and is in the middle of guzzling the whole thing. The Woman glances at her.)* — I think she's all right, she's … wow, really thirsty. *(Juliana sets the water aside, pulls out a carton of Chinese food.)* — Sorry, hold on. — Juliana … *(Juliana is trying to work chopsticks.)* — Juliana, hold on, I'll help you with those. — No she's trying to eat, I think she's starving … — Juliana … — What? Yes I am. On the Cape. *(Another glance at Juliana.)* — Ah, yes, that … that *is* my address. *(Juliana has begun eating the food — albeit as neatly as possible — with a bare hand.)* — OK, this is, is … Well this is … really odd, uh, then I'll … well great. I'll … see you soon, should I throw a fucking dinner party or something? — Sorry. No. Bad joke. OK, I … I guess you don't need directions? OK. *(The Woman hangs up. A beat. She stares at Juliana.)* Juliana? Did you used to live here? In this house?
JULIANA. *(Nodding, eating.)* Mmm. Long time ago. Delicious.
THE WOMAN. Here. Look. You're getting it all over. *(The Woman goes to Juliana, lifts the carton out of her hands. Juliana follows it with her hands.)* Wait wait wait, hang on, hang on, first … *(The Woman sets the container aside, grabs a napkin, takes Juliana's hand, and cleans it.)*

Look up? *(Juliana does. The woman cleans Juliana's face. This is an action that is no-nonsense, and at the same time, one that is supremely caring.)* Good. Now. Here. *(The Woman takes chopsticks, scoops rice and chicken out onto a plate.)*

JULIANA. So hungry.

THE WOMAN. I know, but it's OK. Here. Open. *(Juliana opens. The Woman … feeds her.)* Chew it? *(Juliana does. A small, gentle silence. The Woman watches Juliana eat.)*

JULIANA. Mmm.

THE WOMAN. More? *(Juliana nods and opens her mouth. The Woman feeds her.)*

JULIANA. Who was it on the phone.

THE WOMAN. It was your husband. Ian? He's … apparently right around the corner. *(Off of Juliana's gesture.)* What. Rice? Chicken. Open? Good. It's a … a really … wonderful house.

JULIANA. *(Nodding, chewing.)* Mmm. *(The woman speaks as she continues to feed Juliana, the anonymity of Juliana's memory loss and the intimacy of the moment turning her words into a small, surprisingly personal confession.)*

THE WOMAN. I didn't … ever really think I could fight. So ferociously over something. I mean the thought has crossed my mind that maybe it's because Frank is *such* a prick that I, I, I, just … want to take things from him. I probably should let him *have* the place, the, the life that was going to happen for me here, it's not that life anymore. So I don't really know what I'm holding on to. Anyway, I, I … just wanted to let you know that I've always been able to tell. That this house has been … *(Small beat.)* … this sounds weird, but. Loved. *(Juliana has stopped chewing and is staring at The Woman.)* What is it.

JULIANA. You're not Laurel. Are you. *(A long silence. The Woman stares at Juliana.)*

THE WOMAN. I … *(Long beat. And then she makes a decision.)* am. I'm … Laurel. I'm Laurel. *(Juliana looks at her as if she half believes her.)*

JULIANA. Where did you go that night. *(A beat.)*

THE WOMAN. Um.

JULIANA. Start with you running out of the house.

THE WOMAN. Oh did you have a girl who … Who ran off. Is that what happened to … to … me? *(Juliana nods.)* OK. I … ran. Out of the house.

JULIANA. And then what. Were you hiding out by the road?
THE WOMAN. Uh. Yes. I was. By the road.
JULIANA. So then your father must have driven … right past you.
THE WOMAN. That's right, he … *(The Woman realizes just what it is they're talking about.)* … oh God, you poor woman.
JULIANA. And then did … did Richard come back. Did he or didn't he. He always denied it but I knew in my heart that he took you, because if he didn't take you, who did. And then, if it wasn't him … my God. What horrible things must have happened to you. *(A silence. Something in this affects The Woman deeply.)*
THE WOMAN. Hey. Look at me. Look at me. Nothing … bad. Happened to me.
JULIANA. Well then, why didn't you come back.
THE WOMAN. Because … because everything that happened to me was … so wonderful.
JULIANA. And can you tell me that … wherever you are. You're happy? *(What follows is a deep untruth that is, at the same time, a profoundly earnest fantasy.)*
THE WOMAN. Oh, I'm. I'm so happy. I have … *such* a wonderful life. Richard. And I. We're. We're so happy together. And we're … so in love with the girls. And they can't wait to meet you. I've told them all about you. I've told them how wonderful you are. And I've told them what a … what a wonderful. *Wonderful.* Mother you've been. Mom. *(Juliana sobs. This is the forgiveness she has been waiting so many years to find. The Woman gently puts her arms around Juliana and rocks her.) (Gently.)* It's OK, shh shhhhhhh. It's OK, shh shhhhhhh. It's OK, shh shhhhhhh. It's OK, shh shhhhhhh.
IAN. Hello? *(The Woman dries Juliana's tears. A small beat.)*
THE WOMAN. Your husband's here. *(A small beat. Juliana nods. The Woman gives her a napkin.)* Here. Blow. *(Juliana does. Ian walks in, quietly.)*
IAN. Jules? *(Juliana looks up.)*
JULIANA. Hello sweetheart.
IAN. Is everybody … all right? *(Juliana looks at The Woman.)*
JULIANA. Ian. This young woman. Was just being. Very *kind* to me. *(The Woman helps Juliana stand. For the first time in a long time, Juliana has a moment of profound clarity, as if, for a few seconds, she is the Juliana from long ago.)* I'm … not well, am I.
IAN. … No. You're not.

JULIANA. I … very desperately need help. Don't I.
IAN. You do.
JULIANA. *(Looking around.)* It's very strange to see the other place again.
IAN. Yes it is.
JULIANA. I didn't think I'd ever be back. But obviously it's the place I most want to be.
IAN. Thank you.
JULIANA. You might want to change your locks. *(A beat. Ian puts his arms around Juliana. The Woman exits as The Man enters, as Bobby, Juliana's assistant, and competently preps Juliana for her lecture.)* The first glimmer of it … comes on a Saturday. They've flown us to St. Croix, some private eco-preserve, I now have a child's GPS cell phone with a single number, a nurse/handler who tells me to step here and to stop there; in a few months I will perhaps feel like a curiosity being trotted out of my cage but for now — my first event in six months — the blush is still on the rose. I've been led off the plane, checked in and settled, had my first injection, been given my pill, I've inhaled six pancakes, floated on my back downstairs at the pool; water seems to help me, as do things tactile like working with clay — calm little efforts resulting in the ugly and bizarre which Ian, good Ian, places quietly on the mantle. I finish, I towel off, I flirt with a gaggle of doctors, I go up to shower and dress, the sea is stunning, the air is seventy degrees, I am fifty-three years old, the drapes blow through the windows, and suddenly I feel …
IAN. … What. You feel what. *(Ian enters to join The Man and Juliana.)*
JULIANA. I don't know. I can't explain it.
IAN. Can you try?
JULIANA. … No. It can't be true, I'm just being hopeful.
BOBBY. *(Gently, almost absently, concentrating on his work.)* Why don't you just go ahead and try for him, Juliana.
JULIANA. Well I just feel this morning as if … I'm … as if a … *something*. That was in front of my eyes. Has been lifted.
IAN. *(To Bobby.)* Is that possible?
BOBBY. *(Concentrating.)* I suppose it's possible. It's how she feels.
JULIANA. Well I'm sure I'm making it up, I've just had a good night's sleep so I feel better.
BOBBY. *(Carefully.)* Good days come. And when they do it's very important to be glad for them.

IAN. Or maybe this is how it starts.
JULIANA. I'm sure I'm just being hopeful, this is why you use a, a, whatever —
BOBBY. … Test group? Placebo … ?
JULIANA. Yes; we just want so badly to think we feel better.
IAN. Or maybe this is just how it starts.
BOBBY. Hey, you know? So far, so good.
JULIANA. Am I ready to go.
BOBBY. *(Cleaning up.)* You are.
JULIANA. *(To Ian.)* Will you come down with me. *(Ian looks to Bobby, who stops, nods.)*
IAN. … I think I'll wait up here.
JULIANA. Did that fellow set all my things up.
IAN. Bobby? … Is right here.
JULIANA. *(Embarrassed.)* … Oh.
BOBBY. I've got everything down in the conference room, my name is in a card in your left pocket.
JULIANA. Because I'm still bluffing that I remember things.
BOBBY. … Your right pocket too.
JULIANA. Will you come down with me?
IAN. … I think I'll wait up here. *(Ian and Bobby exit. Juliana carefully references note cards as she speaks. The projection behind her deepens into a brilliant sunset.)*
JULIANA. Gentlemen. Right now. In here. A new version of Identamyl is, we're certain, hard at work. Though neuron death is still occurring, our hope, however, is that it is slowing, or even coming to a halt. Regardless of treatment, the memories I had will never be restored. Neither will my very sense of self, but honestly who am I really if The Great Darkness, as I've begun referring to it, started descending five years ago? Or ten. Or longer. Not being myself is, oddly, who I am. Very rarely, triggered by who knows what, visions — ghosts really — of my past life *do* appear quite vividly. But most often I must settle for memories of *pictures*. Or memories of someone telling me … of *their* memories … of me. I'm also taking a new drug meant to help *clear* these plaques, but because it's made by a competitor, if you ask me what it is … I'll tell you I don't remember. I conclude my lecture. There is applause. There are many conversations I do not retain. I dine quietly with Ian in our room, only dimly realizing this has long been a pleasure of mine. The sun begins to lower. I change into my swimsuit again

and descend, unassisted, into the pool. I float. I breathe. I am a woman in-between: the sky and the earth. The past and the future. This place ... and the other. And then it happens. The water flattens. The sky reddens. The breeze stills. The earth turns. And the girl in the yellow string bikini ... comes back to me. *(An image fills the stage. Juliana turns to watch it. It is a grainy video. A young girl of six or seven runs up to the camera from the beach, then runs back down to the water. She runs back to the camera, waves, then runs back down to the water. The girl's frilly yellow bikini contrasts brightly with the saturated blue of the sea. Juliana watches the girl run and laugh, run and laugh, run and laugh.)*

End of Play

PROPERTY LIST

Notepad, pen
Medical file
2 cups of coffee
Body mic
Cigarettes, lighter
Cell phones
Electric razor
Purse with ballpoint pen
Porcelain bowl with ring
Pad of paper, pen
Cold compress
Briefcase
Glass of water, glass of scotch
Dripping umbrella
Bag of Chinese takeout with large bottle of water, napkins
Cell phone
Purse with wallet
Notecards

SOUND EFFECTS

Children in a bath; screaming, giggling, splashing, crying
Children screaming
Crash of surf
Rain
Door slam
Mahler
Phone rings
Keys, footsteps, door shuts
Cell phone rings

NEW PLAYS

★ **A CIVIL WAR CHRISTMAS: AN AMERICAN MUSICAL CELEBRATION by Paula Vogel, music by Daryl Waters.** It's 1864, and Washington, D.C. is settling down to the coldest Christmas Eve in years. Intertwining many lives, this musical shows us that the gladness of one's heart is the best gift of all. "Boldly inventive theater, warm and affecting." *–Talkin' Broadway.* "Crisp strokes of dialogue." *–NY Times.* [12M, 5W] ISBN: 978-0-8222-2361-0

★ **SPEECH & DEBATE by Stephen Karam.** Three teenage misfits in Salem, Oregon discover they are linked by a sex scandal that's rocked their town. "Savvy comedy." *–Variety.* "Hilarious, cliché-free, and immensely entertaining." *–NY Times.* "A strong, rangy play." *–NY Newsday.* [2M, 2W] ISBN: 978-0-8222-2286-6

★ **DIVIDING THE ESTATE by Horton Foote.** Matriarch Stella Gordon is determined not to divide her 100-year-old Texas estate, despite her family's declining wealth and the looming financial crisis. But her three children have another plan. "Goes for laughs and succeeds." *–NY Daily News.* "The theatrical equivalent of a page-turner." *–Bloomberg.com.* [4M, 9W] ISBN: 978-0-8222-2398-6

★ **WHY TORTURE IS WRONG, AND THE PEOPLE WHO LOVE THEM by Christopher Durang.** Christopher Durang turns political humor upside down with this raucous and provocative satire about America's growing homeland "insecurity." "A smashing new play." *–NY Observer.* "You may laugh yourself silly." *–Bloomberg News.* [4M, 3W] ISBN: 978-0-8222-2401-3

★ **FIFTY WORDS by Michael Weller.** While their nine-year-old son is away for the night on his first sleepover, Adam and Jan have an evening alone together, beginning a suspenseful nightlong roller-coaster ride of revelation, rancor, passion and humor. "Mr. Weller is a bold and productive dramatist." *–NY Times.* [1M, 1W] ISBN: 978-0-8222-2348-1

★ **BECKY'S NEW CAR by Steven Dietz.** Becky Foster is caught in middle age, middle management and in a middling marriage—with no prospects for change on the horizon. Then one night a socially inept and grief-struck millionaire stumbles into the car dealership where Becky works. "Gently and consistently funny." *–Variety.* "Perfect blend of hilarious comedy and substantial weight." *–Broadway Hour.* [4M, 3W] ISBN: 978-0-8222-2393-1

NEW PLAYS

★ **AT HOME AT THE ZOO by Edward Albee.** Edward Albee delves deeper into his play THE ZOO STORY by adding a first act, HOMELIFE, which precedes Peter's fateful meeting with Jerry on a park bench in Central Park. "An essential and heartening experience." –*NY Times.* "Darkly comic and thrilling." –*Time Out.* "Genuinely fascinating." –*Journal News.* [2M, 1W] ISBN: 978-0-8222-2317-7

★ **PASSING STRANGE book and lyrics by Stew, music by Stew and Heidi Rodewald, created in collaboration with Annie Dorsen.** A daring musical about a young bohemian that takes you from black middle-class America to Amsterdam, Berlin and beyond on a journey towards personal and artistic authenticity. "Fresh, exuberant, bracingly inventive, bitingly funny, and full of heart." –*NY Times.* "The freshest musical in town!" –*Wall Street Journal.* "Excellent songs and a vulnerable heart." –*Variety.* [4M, 3W] ISBN: 978-0-8222-2400-6

★ **REASONS TO BE PRETTY by Neil LaBute.** Greg really, truly adores his girlfriend, Steph. Unfortunately, he also thinks she has a few physical imperfections, and when he mentions them, all hell breaks loose. "Tight, tense and emotionally true." –*Time Magazine.* "Lively and compulsively watchable." –*The Record.* [2M, 2W] ISBN: 978-0-8222-2394-8

★ **OPUS by Michael Hollinger.** With only a few days to rehearse a grueling Beethoven masterpiece, a world-class string quartet struggles to prepare their highest-profile performance ever—a televised ceremony at the White House. "Intimate, intense and profoundly moving." –*Time Out.* "Worthy of scores of bravissimos." –*BroadwayWorld.com.* [4M, 1W] ISBN: 978-0-8222-2363-4

★ **BECKY SHAW by Gina Gionfriddo.** When an evening calculated to bring happiness takes a dark turn, crisis and comedy ensue in this wickedly funny play that asks what we owe the people we love and the strangers who land on our doorstep. "As engrossing as it is ferociously funny." –*NY Times.* "Gionfriddo is some kind of genius." –*Variety.* [2M, 3W] ISBN: 978-0-8222-2402-0

★ **KICKING A DEAD HORSE by Sam Shepard.** Hobart Struther's horse has just dropped dead. In an eighty-minute monologue, he discusses what path brought him here in the first place, the fate of his marriage, his career, politics and eventually the nature of the universe. "Deeply instinctual and intuitive." –*NY Times.* "The brilliance is in the infinite reverberations Shepard extracts from his simple metaphor." –*TheaterMania.* [1M, 1W] ISBN: 978-0-8222-2336-8

NEW PLAYS

★ **AUGUST: OSAGE COUNTY by Tracy Letts.** WINNER OF THE 2008 PULITZER PRIZE AND TONY AWARD. When the large Weston family reunites after Dad disappears, their Oklahoma homestead explodes in a maelstrom of repressed truths and unsettling secrets. "Fiercely funny and bitingly sad." *–NY Times.* "Ferociously entertaining." *–Variety.* "A hugely ambitious, highly combustible saga." *–NY Daily News.* [6M, 7W] ISBN: 978-0-8222-2300-9

★ **RUINED by Lynn Nottage.** WINNER OF THE 2009 PULITZER PRIZE. Set in a small mining town in Democratic Republic of Congo, RUINED is a haunting, probing work about the resilience of the human spirit during times of war. "A full-immersion drama of shocking complexity and moral ambiguity." *–Variety.* "Sincere, passionate, courageous." *–Chicago Tribune.* [8M, 4W] ISBN: 978-0-8222-2390-0

★ **GOD OF CARNAGE by Yasmina Reza, translated by Christopher Hampton.** WINNER OF THE 2009 TONY AWARD. A playground altercation between boys brings together their Brooklyn parents, leaving the couples in tatters as the rum flows and tensions explode. "Satisfyingly primitive entertainment." *–NY Times.* "Elegant, acerbic, entertainingly fueled on pure bile." *–Variety.* [2M, 2W] ISBN: 978-0-8222-2399-3

★ **THE SEAFARER by Conor McPherson.** Sharky has returned to Dublin to look after his irascible, aging brother. Old drinking buddies Ivan and Nicky are holed up at the house too, hoping to play some cards. But with the arrival of a stranger from the distant past, the stakes are raised ever higher. "Dark and enthralling Christmas fable." *–NY Times.* "A timeless classic." *–Hollywood Reporter.* [5M] ISBN: 978-0-8222-2284-2

★ **THE NEW CENTURY by Paul Rudnick.** When the playwright is Paul Rudnick, expectations are geared for a play both hilarious and smart, and this provocative and outrageous comedy is no exception. "The one-liners fly like rockets." *–NY Times.* "The funniest playwright around." *–Journal News.* [2M, 3W] ISBN: 978-0-8222-2315-3

★ **SHIPWRECKED! AN ENTERTAINMENT—THE AMAZING ADVENTURES OF LOUIS DE ROUGEMONT (AS TOLD BY HIMSELF) by Donald Margulies.** The amazing story of bravery, survival and celebrity that left nineteenth-century England spellbound. Dare to be whisked away. "A deft, literate narrative." *–LA Times.* "Springs to life like a theatrical pop-up book." *–NY Times.* [2M, 1W] ISBN: 978-0-8222-2341-2